go crazy with
Duct Tape

DUCK®

LEISURE ARTS, INC.
Little Rock, Arkansas

EDITORIAL STAFF
Vice President and Editor-in-Chief:
   Susan White Sullivan
Special Projects Director: Susan Frantz Wiles
Director of E-Commerce: Mark Hawkins
Art Publications Director: Rhonda Shelby
Special Projects Designer: Patti Wallenfang
Technical Writer: Mary Sullivan Hutcheson
Technical Associate: Jean Lewis
Editorial Writer: Susan McManus Johnson
Art Category Manager: Lora Puls
Senior Publications Designer: Dana Vaughn
Graphic Artists: Dayle Carroza,
   Jacob Castleton, Kara Darling, and
   Stacy Owens
Imaging Technician: Stephanie Johnson
Prepress Technician: Janie Marie Wright
Photography Manager: Katherine Laughlin
Contributing Photographer: Ken West
Contributing Photo Stylists: Sondra Daniel
   and Brooke Duszota
Manager of E-Commerce: Robert Young

BUSINESS STAFF
President and Chief Executive Officer:
   Rick Barton
Vice President of Sales: Mike Behar
Vice President of Finance:
   Laticia Mull Dittrich
National Sales Director: Martha Adams
Creative Services: Chaska Lucas
Information Technology Director:
   Hermine Linz
Controller: Francis Caple
Vice President, Operations: Jim Dittrich
Retail Customer Service Manager:
   Stan Raynor
Vice President of Purchasing: Fred F. Pruss

ISBN-13: 978-1-46470-458-1

Contents

Wake up your world with today's duct tape! Use those cool colors to design your own jewelry and all kinds of bags. You can customize a suitcase, a pair of boots, a video game guitar—even a recliner! Lots of photos and the basic how-tos make it easy to finish all these fantastic ideas. Duct tape creativity is So. Much. Fun!

DUCK® vs. duct

For the record... DUCK® is the brand of tape that is featured in this book, and is a registered trademark of ShurTech Brands, LLC, Avon, OH.

Duct tape is the generic product description for the type of tape used in this book.

Only duct tape distributed by ShurTech Brands, LLC has the right to be called "DUCK TAPE®". When shopping for your duct tape, be sure to look for the Trust E. Duck logo (shown below) to ensure you are getting the original DUCK® brand quality!

3

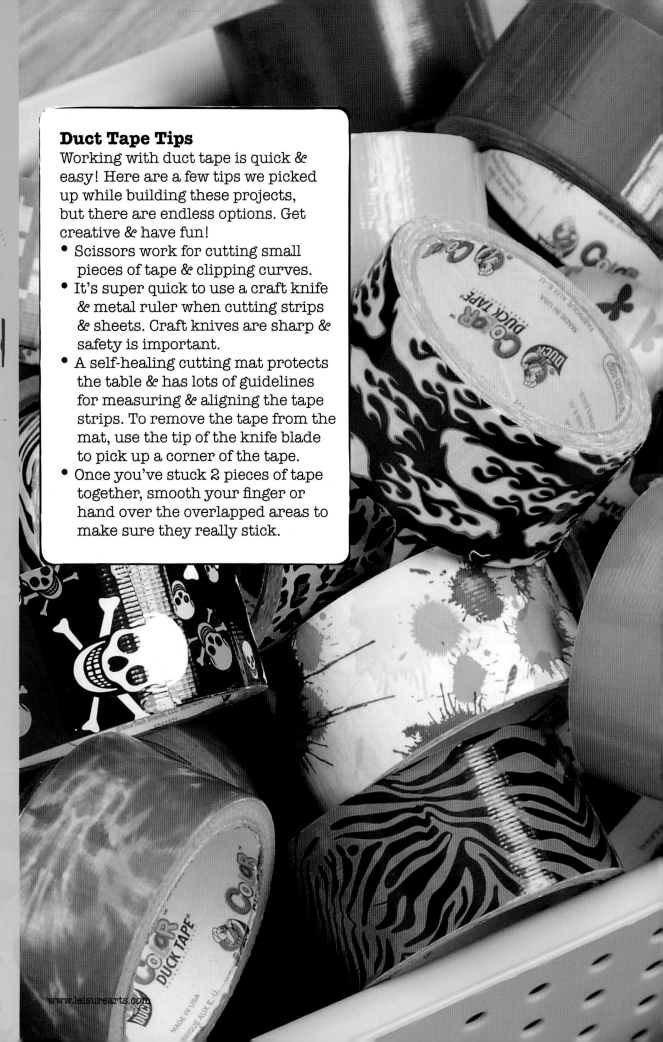

Duct Tape Tips

Working with duct tape is quick & easy! Here are a few tips we picked up while building these projects, but there are endless options. Get creative & have fun!

- Scissors work for cutting small pieces of tape & clipping curves.
- It's super quick to use a craft knife & metal ruler when cutting strips & sheets. Craft knives are sharp & safety is important.
- A self-healing cutting mat protects the table & has lots of guidelines for measuring & aligning the tape strips. To remove the tape from the mat, use the tip of the knife blade to pick up a corner of the tape.
- Once you've stuck 2 pieces of tape together, smooth your finger or hand over the overlapped areas to make sure they really stick.

Making a Single-Sided Sheet

Stick the tape end to a cutting mat & roll out. Cut the strip from the roll.

Stick a second strip to the mat, overlapping the first. Keep adding strips until you have the right size sheet.

Cut the strips a bit longer than you need; then, trim the sheet.

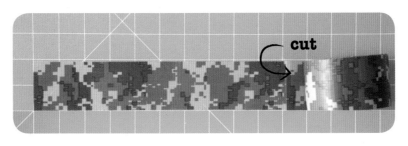

cut

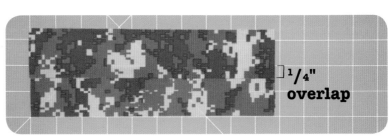

1/4" overlap

Making a Double-Sided Sheet

Make 2 Single-Sided Sheets. Stick the sheets to each other.

Cut the strips a bit longer than you need. After sticking the sheets together, trim to size.

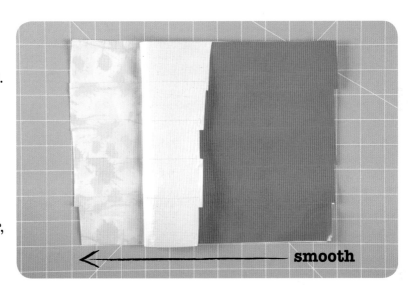

smooth

Making an Offset Strip

Cut 2 strips of tape & stick to each other, offsetting the top strip.

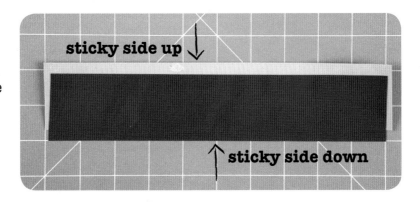

sticky side up ↓

sticky side down

Making a Double-Sided Strip

Cut 2 strips of tape & stick to each other

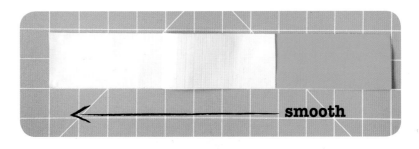

smooth

Basics

5

Making a Plastic-Lined Single-Sided Sheet

Make a Single-Sided Sheet (page 5). Stick the sheet to a clear plastic drop cloth or garbage bag. Trim the sheet to size.

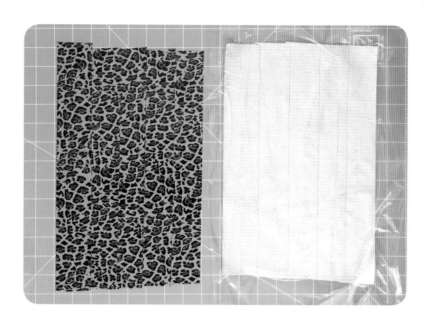

Covering An Edge

Trim a piece of tape to the desired width. The projects use 1", 1¹/₂", & the whole tape width. Place the edge about halfway over the tape; fold the tape down.

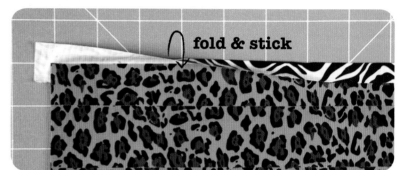

fold & stick

Making Covered Yarn

Cut a tape strip & lay a piece of yarn along the edge. Tightly roll until the yarn is covered.

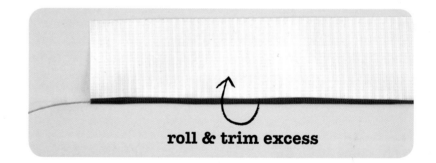

roll & trim excess

Making a Strap

Cut a tape strip the indicated length. Trim the width (see page 7). Place the tape, sticky side up, on the cutting mat. Fold one long edge about ¹/₃ of the way toward the middle.

fold about ¹/₃ up

Fold down the other long edge & smooth.

fold & stick

smooth

www.leisurearts.com

Covering A Button

 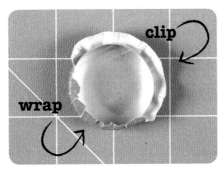 

Covered button kits come with 2 pieces.

Stick tape to the domed side of the button. Clip the curves & wrap the tape to the inside.

Push the bottom into the button.

Making Tape Appliqués

  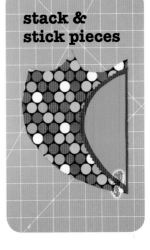

Trace the patterns onto paper & cut out.

Make a Single-Sided Sheet (on non-stick foil) to fit the pattern. Draw around the pattern on the sheet; cut out the appliqué and peel away the foil. Stick the appliqué on your project.

For stacked appliqués, like the owl, stack the smaller appliqué pieces on the larger ones on a cutting mat. Then stick the whole thing on your project.

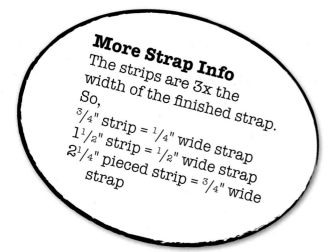

More Strap Info

The strips are 3x the width of the finished strap. So,

$3/4$" strip = $1/4$" wide strap
$1 1/2$" strip = $1/2$" wide strap
$2 1/4$" pieced strip = $3/4$" wide strap

Necklaces

Get a bag of small wood shapes & cover the squares with tape. Punch holes.

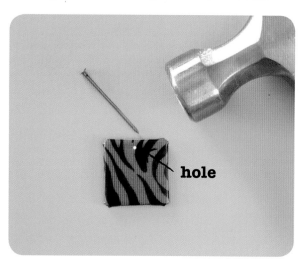

hole

Thread ribbons & cords through the holes, adding beads, buttons, charms, or straw segments. Add a stick-on jeweled intial for each of your friends.

Rings

Make a strap (page 6). Tape into a ring.

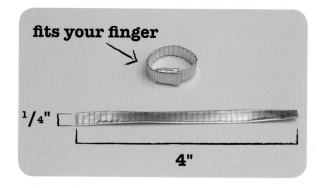

fits your finger

1/4"

4"

Cut a cardboard "stone" & cover with tape. Tape the stone to the ring.

tape here

Wrap the stone & ring with thin copper & gold wires. Cover the wires with tape on the inside.

add more tape

Jewelry

Make the best bling for your friends! It's so easy!

Earrings

First, get a bag of small wood shapes. Then, cover 2 shapes with tape. Punch holes. Add earring wires & some sparkle.

Jewelry Boxes

Trim plain white boxes with tape strips & self-adhesive jewels to make fun gift boxes.

Bangle Bracelets

Add some tape to bangles. Stick on some jewels for sparkle. Or, stick tape to non-stick foil & punch out circles to decorate the bracelet. Let the bracelet size, shape, & color inspire you!

clip

wrap

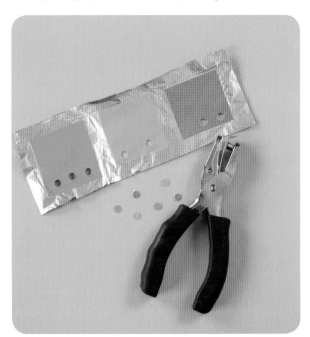

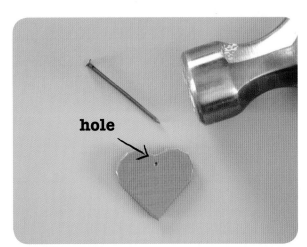

hole

Have fun being your own jewelry designer!

Tape-Wad Bracelet

Cut some elastic cord. Gently wad up scraps of tape & wrap around the cord, adding beads between the wads.

Tie on pretty charms & pieces of old necklaces & earrings. Knot the cord ends together.

Stretchy Bracelets

Wrap straws with tape.

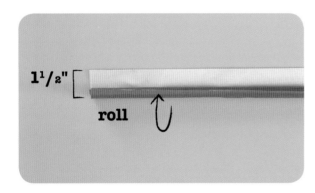

1¹/₂" [

roll

Cut the covered straws into short pieces. Thread onto an elastic cord with a large-eye, sharp needle. You can also use beads & double-sided tape squares for your bracelet. Knot the cord ends together.

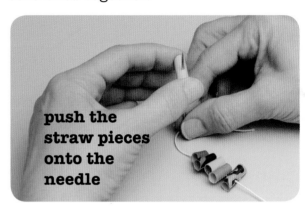

push the straw pieces onto the needle

all straw pieces

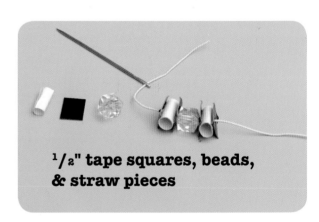

¹/₂" tape squares, beads, & straw pieces

Cover straws
with tape for
crazy beaded
bracelets!

13

Before

"Leather" Vest

Trim the fronts from a resale shop vest. Cover a cutting mat with torn pieces of tan tape, overlapping & placing the pieces any which way.

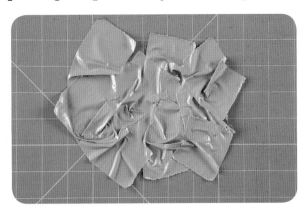

Rub walnut-colored gel stain into the tape. Let dry overnight; then, rub down with a cloth to make sure it is completely dry.

Use the vest fronts as patterns to cut the tape. Line the tape fronts with clear plastic (page 6).

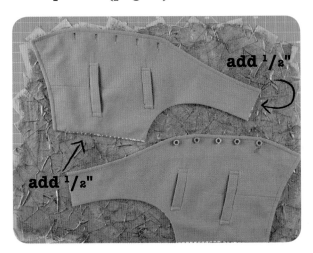

add ¹/₂"

add ¹/₂"

Staple the tape fronts to the vest back at the side & shoulder seams. Cover the seams with tape.

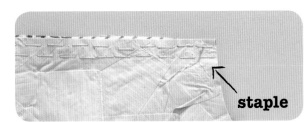

staple

tape & trim

After

Overlap brown tape pieces to make "Duck®-pleather"!

Before

Ribbon-Tied Vest

Refer to the photos on page 14 when making the vest.

Make a plastic-lined single-sided sheet (page 6). Cut the fronts off a resale shop vest. Use the fronts as patterns to cut the tape sheet.

Staple the tape fronts to the vest back at the side & shoulder seams.

Cover the seams with tape.

Add tape pieces to fronts; slit & add ribbon ties.

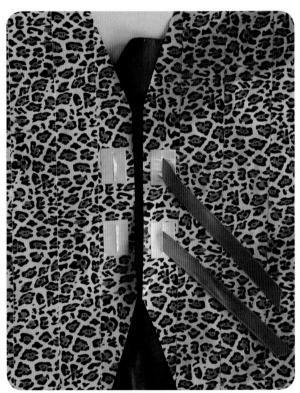

Just tape, staple, & add ties! It's ready to wear!

After

Funky Chunky Boots
Stick tape strips to some funky resale shop boots.

Peacock Boots
Use the peacock feather pattern to make tape appliqués (page 7). Add the details lines with a black marker. Stick the appliqués on your boots.

Leisure Arts, Inc. grants permission to the owner of this book to copy the pattern on this page for personal use only.

Cute boots! Make them feathered or funky !

Sunglasses

For the striped shades, cut tiny tape strips & stick on the lenses.

For the dotted shades, stick some tape pieces on non-stick foil & punch out small circles. Stick the circles on the lenses.

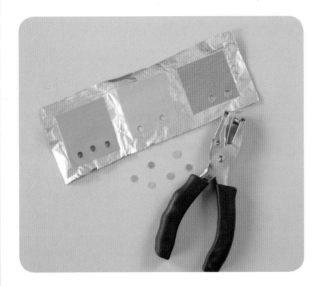

Sunglasses Case

Use your sunglasses to make a paper pattern. Use narrow strips of tape to make a double-sided sheet (page 5) the same size.

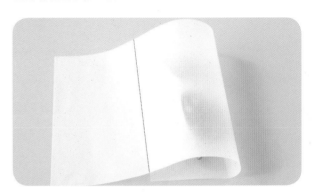

Cover the top edge (page 6).

Fold the sheet in half & cover the bottom & side edges.

Phone Case

Use your phone to make a paper pattern. Use narrow strips of tape to make a double-sided sheet (page 5) the same size.

Cover the top edge (page 6). Fold & tape the sheet at the back. Cover the bottom edge.

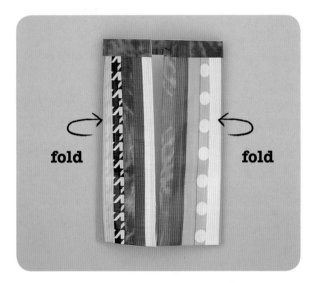

fold   fold

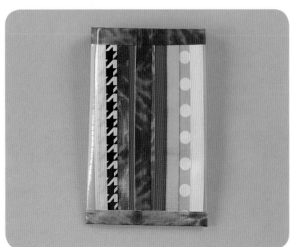

Belts

For the ring belt, make ¹/₂" x 6" straps (page 6). Thread the straps through the rings & tape.

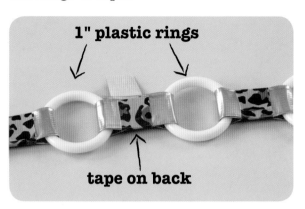

1" plastic rings

tape on back

To make the ties, cut some yarn & cover with tape (page 6). Add the ties to the last ring on each side of the belt.

wrap with tape

For the grommeted belt, cut ¹/₂" tape strips. Run the strips through the grommets & tape to the belt.

tape down on back

Make a sassy belt with rings & yarn, or just add tape!

Invitation

Cover cardboard rolls with tape; cover the edges (page 6).

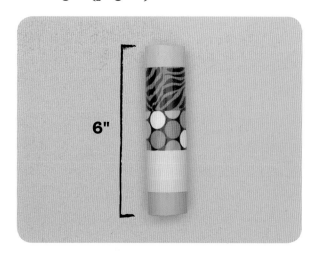

Make a double-sided flame tape strip (page 5). Cut candle flame shapes. Tape the flames to straws.

use pattern to cut shapes

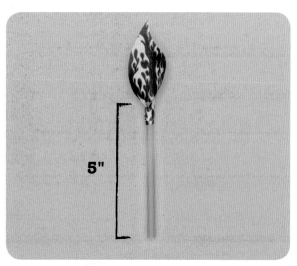

5"

Roll up the invitation, some tissue paper, & a flame. Insert in the taped roll.

roll up & insert

Make a double-sided tape strip & punch out circle tags. Write your message on the tags. Cover a piece of yarn (page 6) & use it to hang the tag from the cardboard roll.

LOOK inside!

Let's PARTY HEARTY!

Ask friends to your party with candle invitations!

Thanks!

Thanks!

Thanks!

25

Party Cups

Wrap a tape strip around plastic party cups.

Favors

Pop a hole in the wrapping of a roll of tape. Fill the hole with candy.

For the twistie, wrap a chenille stem with tape.

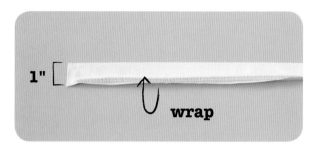

1" **wrap**

For the tag, make a double-sided tape strip. Write "Thanks" on the tag.

Wrap the roll of tape in cellophane & tie up with the twistie, adding the tag.

punched hole

Thanks! :)

trim with wavy scissors

Duck® Tape
adds fun to
party cups and
favors!

Thanks!

Thanks!

Recliner

Take an old vinyl or leather recliner & replace any missing padding or stuffing with quilt batting.

Cover the large areas of the recliner with a busy overall print, like the leopard print. Short, overlapping pieces of tape work best on the curved areas.

Have fun covering the rest of the recliner with all the great tape colors & patterns that are available!

Before

Wallet

Make a double-sided sheet (page 5).
Fold the sheet; tape the sides together.

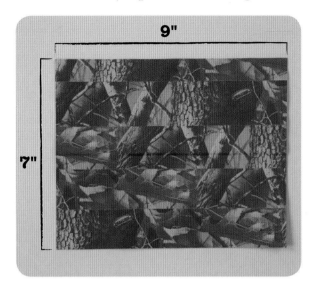

9"

7"

Make a 15" double-sided tape strip
(page 5). Cover the top edge (page 6)
& cut 4 pockets.

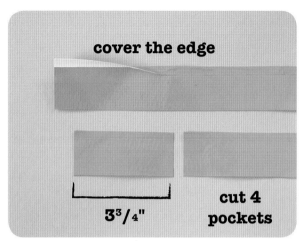

cover the edge

3³/₄"

cut 4
pockets

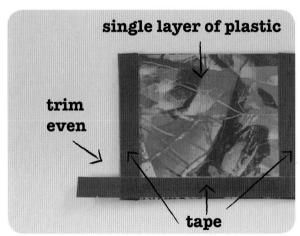

tape here & here

Stack the pockets & tape to the wallet.
Fold in half.

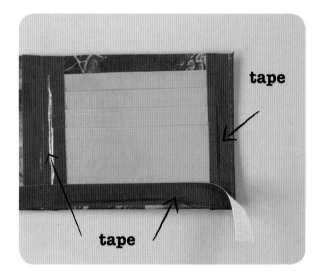

tape

tape

Add a clear plastic badge holder.

single layer of plastic

trim
even

tape

All guys need a camo wallet! Dude, where'd it go?

Message Suitcase

Spray a suitcase silver. Print out "not yours" in a large font.

Cover the suitcase with tape. Add contrasting strips & stick "not yours" on with clear tape.

Owl Suitcase

Make tape appliqués (page 7) with the patterns on pages 47-48. Cut some pieces with scallop-edged scissors.

Cover 1" dia. buttons (page 7). Stick the appliqués on the suitcase, glue on the eyes & trim the suitcase edges with strips of tape.

Before

Use Duck® Tape to create a 'case like no other!

After

Recycled Cans & Boxes

Cover or trim cans, old tins & even oatmeal boxes with strips of tape. Add some beaded trims, a ruffled tape flower, or a handle.

For the ruffled flower, make 2 different offset strips, folding the top edge down (page 5). Fold & pleat each strip onto itself.

Glue the ruffled flower pieces to a tin lid & add a jewel at the center.

For a handle, make a $^3/_4$" x 14" strap (page 6) & tape to the can.

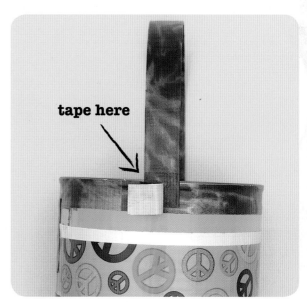

tape here

fold & pleat into a circle

Cans & boxes get amazing with Duck® Tape!

Toolbox

Get a toolbox & cover the handle with tape.

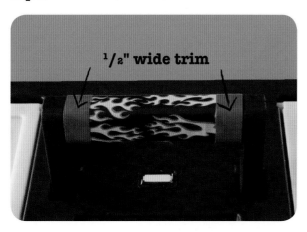

Add some tape to the box front, too.

Guitar

Cover the large areas of a gaming guitar with tape.

Add chrome tape accents to the guitar.

Photo Album

Make a single-sided sheet (page 5) to cover most of the album front. Cover the edges (page 6).

Make another single-sided sheet to cover the inside.

Guy Stuff

Flame tape—
a hot idea for
making things
cool!

37

Candles

Wrap plain candle jars with tape for a quick gift.

Monogram

Make a single-sided sheet (page 5). Stick the sheet to a wooden letter & trim the excess.

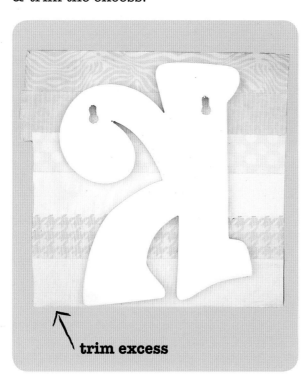

trim excess

Bookmarks

Make a $^1/_2$" x 7" strap (page 6). Thread the strap through a giant paperclip & wrap with tape.

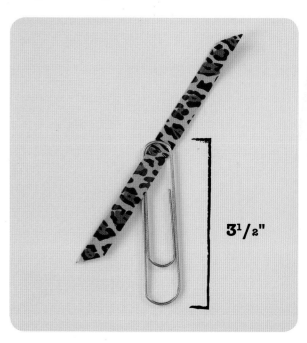

$3^1/_2$"

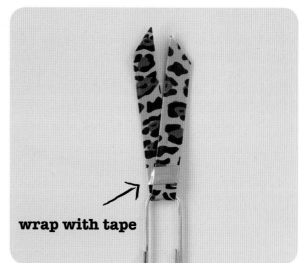

wrap with tape

Gifts

Great gifts for your friends & family! So fun & easy!

Bulletin Board

Cover the edges of a bulletin board (page 6) & add a center stripe.

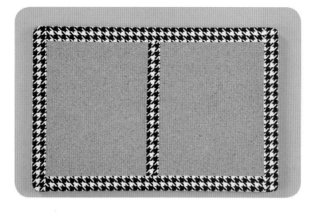

Make a double-sided sheet (page 5) for the flower petals. Use the pattern (page 47) to cut the petals.

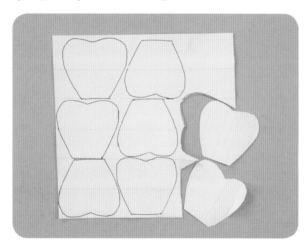

For the ruffled center, make an off-set strip, folding the top edge down (page 5). Pleat & fold the strip into a circle.

For the fringed middle, make an off-set strip, folding the top edge down. Cut the fringe; then, pleat & fold the strip into a circle.

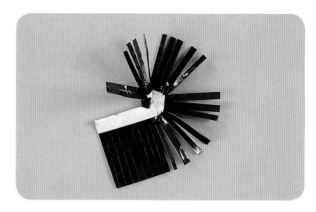

Cover a 1½" dia. button (page 7).

Glue the petals to the bulletin board, slitting & overlapping the 2nd layer of petals.

Glue the ruffled center, fringed middle, & covered button to the board.

Hanger

Wrap tape strips around a hanger.

Make a big, sassy bloom to brighten your room!

Zippered Bags

Make 2 lined single-sided sheets (page 6).

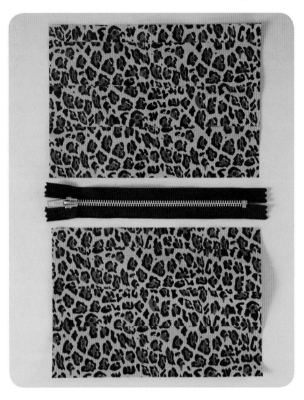

Cover the side & bottom edges (page 6) with tape.

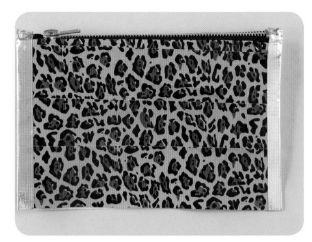

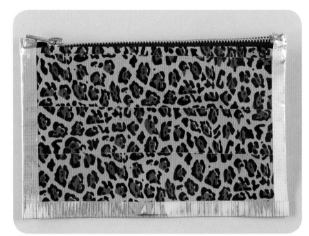

Staple the sheets to the zipper.

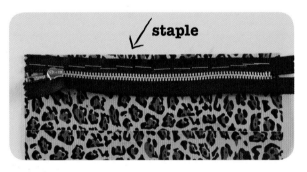

staple

Make a ¹/₂" x 3" strap (page 6). Tape to the corner.

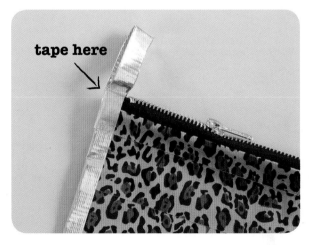

tape here

Flatten & cover the stapled edges with tape.

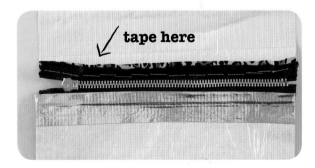

tape here

Just stick & staple these handy bags!

Tote Bag

Trim the zipper from a food storage bag.

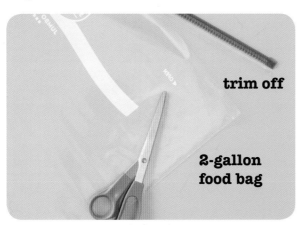

trim off

2-gallon food bag

Make 2 single-sided sheets (page 5) & stick the sheets to the bag front & back.

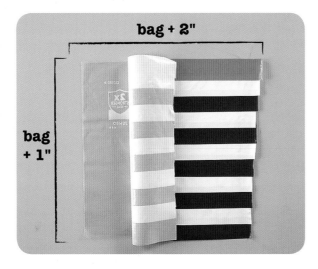

bag + 2"

bag + 1"

Press the side & bottom edges together; then, trim off ¹/₂".

trim off ¹/₂"

Cover the bottom & top edges (page 6).

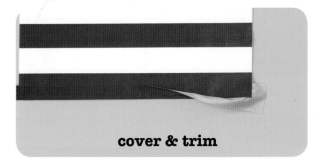

cover & trim

For the handles, add orange stripes & rings to both sides of the bag.

1" ring

Make two ³/₄" x 24" straps (page 6) & thread through the rings.

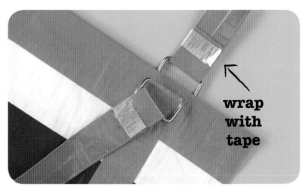

wrap with tape

www.leisurearts.com

Your fun gear is ready to go in an awesome beach bag!

Beach Mat

Cover the edges (page 6) of a bamboo beach mat with tape.

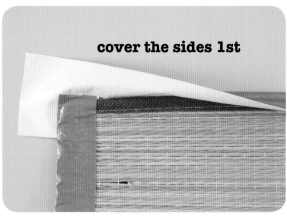

Make a $^1/_2$" x 22" strap (page 6) & tape to the mat.

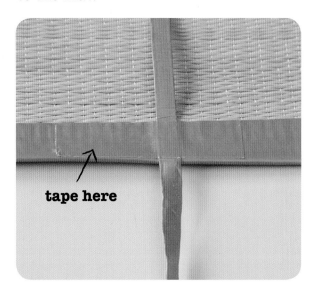

Covered Water Bottle

Wrap an aluminum water bottle with tape strips.

Soccer Ball

Trace one of the colored shapes on paper.

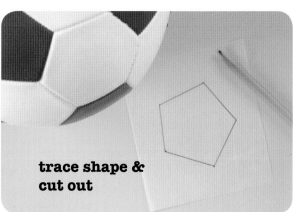

Make tape appliqués (page 7) & stick on the ball.

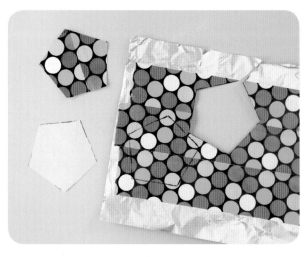

bulletin board petal

suitcase owl

patterns

suitcase owl cont.

overlap pink dots
to complete branch
pattern

www.leisurearts.com